100 facts

PLANET EARTH

100 facts
PLANET EARTH

Peter Riley

Consultant: Clive Carpenter

Miles Kelly

First published in 2002 by Miles Kelly Publishing Ltd
Harding's Barn, Bardfield End Green, Thaxted, Essex, CM6 3PX, UK

Copyright © Miles Kelly Publishing 2002

This edition updated 2013, printed in 2014

6 8 10 9 7 5

Publishing Director Belinda Gallagher
Creative Director Jo Cowan
Editorial Director Rosie Neave
Assistant Editor Amy Johnson
Designers Rob Hale, John Christopher (White Design), Venita Kidwai
Production Manager Elizabeth Collins
Reprographics Stephan Davis, Jennifer Cozens, Thom Allaway
Assets Lorraine King

ISBN 978-1-78209-195-0

Printed in China

British Library Cataloguing-in-Publication Data
A catalogue record for this book is available from the British Library

ACKNOWLEDGEMENTS
The publishers would like to thank the following sources for the use of their photographs:
Key: t = top, b = bottom, c = centre, l = left, r = right, m = main

Cover (front) Vlue/Shutterstock, (back, t) szefei/Shutterstock, (cl) Mirkamoksha/Dreamstime, (cr) Johan Swanepoel
Corbis 15 Douglas Peebles; 18(t) Craig Tuttle; 21(m) Jeff Vanuga; 28(m) Lloyd Cluff; 32(tr) Michael S. Yamashita
Dreamstime 23(tr) Mirkamoksha **FLPA** 38(m) Phil McLean; 39(t) Michael & Patricia Fogden/Minden Pictures
Fotolia paper (throughout) Konstantin Sutyagin, Anette Linnea Rasmus; graph paper (throughout) Sharpshot; 25(t) (blue paper)
Alexey Khromushin; 42(c) (yellow paper) U.P.images **iStock** 16(m) Lukáš Hejtman; 23(m) IMPALASTOCK; 26(m); weareadventurers
NASA 9(tr) **Shutterstock** 1 and 37(t) Oliver Klimek; 2–3 somchaij; 5(b) Pichugin Dmitry; 10–11 Alexey Repka; 11(bl) Wild Arctic Pictures,
(cr) Snowbelle; 13(b) Sam DCruz; 18(b) Jose Gil; 19(m) Jarno Gonzalez Zarraonandia; 20(m) Becky Stares; 24(b) yvon52; 25(c) urosr,
(b) Crepesoles; 29(tl) Menna, (tc) Spirit of America, (tr) yankane; 31(tr) MarcelClemens, (br) douglas knight; 32(l) Denis Selivanov;
35(m) Todd Shoemake, (t) Vladislav Gurfinkel, (b) Kichigin; 39(b) Steve Bower; 40(b) Vadim Petrakov; 41(b) Willem Tims;
43(l) Rich Carey; 44(t) Krzysztof Odziomek, (b) Cathy Keifer

All other photographs are from:
digitalSTOCK, digitalvision, ImageState, iStockphoto.com,
John Foxx, PhotoAlto, PhotoDisc, PhotoEssentials, PhotoPro, Stockbyte

All artworks are from the Miles Kelly Artwork Bank

Every effort has been made to acknowledge the source and copyright holder of each picture.
Miles Kelly Publishing apologizes for any unintentional errors or omissions.

Made with paper from a sustainable forest

www.mileskelly.net
info@mileskelly.net

Contents

The speedy space ball

1 The Earth is a huge ball of rock moving through space at nearly 3000 metres per second. It weighs 6000 million, million, million tonnes. Up to two-thirds of the Earth's rocky surface is covered by water – this makes up the seas and oceans. Rock that is not covered by water makes up the land. Surrounding the Earth is a layer of gases called the atmosphere (air). This reaches to about 1000 kilometres above the Earth's surface – then space begins.

▶ Earth and the planets nearest to it in the Solar System. Mercury, the planet closest to the Sun, is small and hot. Venus and Earth are rocky and cooler.

VENUS

MERCURY

SUN

MOON

EARTH

Where did Earth come from?

2 **The Earth came from a cloud in space.** Scientists think it formed from a huge cloud of gas and dust around 4500 million years ago. A star near the cloud exploded, making the cloud spin. As the cloud span, gases gathered at its centre and formed the Sun. Dust whizzed around the Sun and began to stick together to form lumps of rock. In time, the rocks crashed into each other and made the planets. The Earth is one of these planets.

⑤ The Earth was made up of one large piece of land, now split into seven chunks known as continents

① Cloud starts to spin

▶ Clouds of gas and dust are made from the remains of old stars that have exploded or run out of energy. It is from these clouds that new stars and planets form.

④ Volcanoes erupt, releasing gases, helping to form the early atmosphere

③ The Earth begins to cool and a hard shell forms

3 **At first the Earth was very hot.** As the rocks collided they heated each other up. Later, as the Earth formed, the rocks inside it melted. The new Earth was a ball of liquid rock with a thin, solid shell.

② Dust gathers into lumps of rock that form a small planet

4 Huge numbers of large rocks called meteorites crashed into the Earth. They made round hollows on the surface. These hollows are called craters. The Moon was hit with meteorites at the same time. Look at the Moon with binoculars – you can see the craters that were made long ago.

▶ The Moon was hit by meteorites, which made huge craters and mountain ranges up to 5000 metres high.

▼ Erupting volcanoes and fierce storms helped form the atmosphere and oceans. These provided energy that was needed for life on Earth to begin.

5 The seas and oceans formed as the Earth cooled down. Volcanoes erupted, letting out steam, gases and rocks. As the Earth cooled, the steam changed to water droplets and formed clouds. As the Earth cooled further, rain fell from the clouds. It took millions of years of rain to form the seas and oceans.

I DON'T BELIEVE IT!

Millions of rocks crash into Earth as it speeds through space. Some larger ones may reach the ground as meteorites.

In a spin

6 **The Earth is like a spinning top.** It continues to spin because it was formed from a spinning cloud of gas and dust. The Earth turns around an invisible line called an axis. It does not spin straight up but leans to one side. The Earth takes 24 hours to spin around once – we call this period of time a day.

▲ As one half of the Earth turns towards sunlight, the other half turns towards darkness. It is morning when one half turns into sunlight, and evening as the other half turns into darkness.

7 **Spinning makes day and night.** Each part of the Earth spins towards the Sun, and then away from it every day. When a part of the Earth is facing the Sun it is daytime there. When that part is facing away from the Sun it is nighttime. Is the Earth facing the Sun or facing away from it where you are?

8

The Earth spins around two points on its surface. They are at opposite ends of the planet. One is at the top of the Earth, called the North Pole. The other is at the bottom of the Earth. It is called the South Pole. The North and South Poles are covered by ice and snow all year round.

9

The spinning Earth acts like a magnet. At the centre of the Earth is liquid iron. As the Earth spins, it makes the iron behave like a magnet with a North and South Pole. These act on the magnet in a compass to make the needle point to the North and South Poles.

North Pole

▼ If you were in space and looked at the Earth from the side, it would appear to move from left to right. If you looked down on Earth from the North Pole, it would seem to be moving anticlockwise.

Direction of Earth's spin

Axis

South Pole

▲ The region around the North Pole is called the Arctic. It consists of the Arctic Ocean, which is mainly covered in a layer of floating ice.

▼ These lines show the pulling power of the magnet inside the Earth.

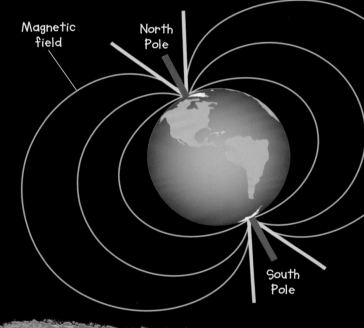

Magnetic field

North Pole

South Pole

MAKE A COMPASS

You will need:
bowl of water   piece of wood
bar magnet   real compass

Place the wood in the water with the magnet on top. Make sure they do not touch the sides. When the wood is still, check which way the magnet is pointing with your compass, by placing it on a flat surface. It will tell you the direction of the Poles.

Inside the Earth

10 There are different layers inside the Earth. There is a thin, rocky crust on the surface, a solid middle called the mantle and a centre called the core. The outer core is liquid but the inner part of the core is solid metal.

11 At the centre of the Earth is a huge metal ball called the inner core. It is 2500 kilometres wide and is made mainly from iron, with some nickel. The ball has an incredible temperature of around 7000°C – hot enough to make the metals melt. However, they stay solid because the other layers of the Earth push down heavily on them.

12 Around the centre of the Earth flows a hot, liquid layer of iron and nickel. This layer is the outer core and is about 2200 kilometres thick. As the Earth spins, the inner and outer core move at different speeds.

13 The largest layer is called the mantle. It is around 2900 kilometres thick. It lies between the core and the crust. The mantle is made of soft, hot rock. In the upper mantle, near the crust, the rock moves more slowly.

Atmosphere

Crust

Mantle
4500°C

Outer core
5000°C

Inner core
7000°C

◄ The internal structure of the Earth. The centre of the Earth – the inner core – is solid even though it is intensely hot. This is because it is under extreme pressure.

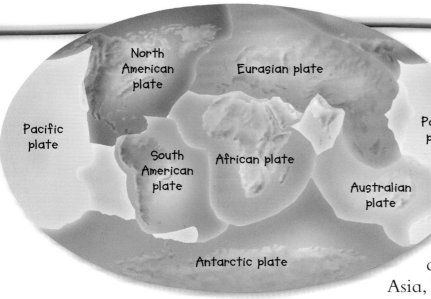

North American plate

Eurasian plate

Pacific plate

Pacific plate

South American plate

African plate

Australian plate

Antarctic plate

▲ Six of the seven tectonic plates carry a continent. The Pacific plate does not.

15 The crust is divided into huge slabs of rock called tectonic plates. The plates all have both land and seas on top of them except for the Pacific plate, which is just covered by water. The large areas of land on the plates are called continents. There are seven continents in total – Africa, Asia, Europe, North America, South America, Oceania and Antarctica.

14 The Earth's surface is covered by crust. Land is made of continental crust between 20 and 70 kilometres thick. Most of this is made from a rock called granite. The ocean bed is made of oceanic crust about eight kilometres thick. It is made mainly from a rock called basalt.

▼ The Great Rift Valley in Kenya is part of a huge system of rift valleys. It is the result of tectonic plates moving apart, causing the Earth's crust to separate.

16 Very, very slowly, the continents are moving. Slow-flowing mantle under the crust moves the tectonic plates across the Earth's surface. As the plates move, so do the continents. In some places, the plates push into each other. In others, they move apart. North America is moving three centimetres away from Europe every year!

Hot rocks

17 There are places on Earth where hot, liquid rocks shoot up through the surface. These are volcanoes. Beneath a volcano is a huge space filled with molten (liquid) rock. This is the magma chamber. Inside the chamber, pressure builds like the pressure in a fizzy drink's can if you shake it. Ash, steam and molten rock called lava escape from the top of the volcano – this is an eruption.

Lava flowing away from vent

Molten rock spreading out under the volcano and cooling down

Volcanic bomb

▶ When a volcano erupts, the hot rock from inside the Earth escapes as ash, smoke, lumps of rock called volcanic bombs and rivers of lava.

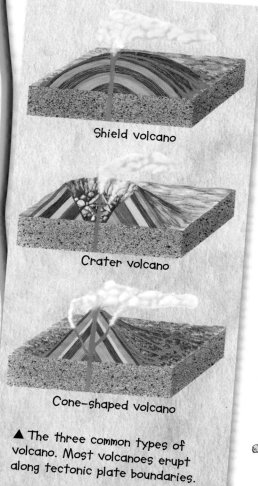

Shield volcano

Crater volcano

Cone-shaped volcano

▲ The three common types of volcano. Most volcanoes erupt along tectonic plate boundaries.

18 Volcanoes erupt in different ways and form different shapes. Most have a central 'pipe', reaching from the magma chamber up to the vent opening. Some volcanoes have runny lava. It flows from the vent and makes a domed shape called a shield volcano. Other volcanoes have thick lava. When they erupt, gases in the lava make it explode into pieces of ash. The ash settles on the lava to make a cone-shaped volcano. A caldera, or crater volcano, is made when the top of a cone-shaped volcano explodes and sinks into the magma chamber.

Cloud of ash, steam and smoke

Layers of rock from previous eruptions

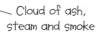**19** **There are volcanoes under the sea.** Where tectonic plates move apart, lava flows out from rift volcanoes to fill the gap. The hot lava is cooled quickly by the sea and forms pillow-shaped lumps called pillow lava.

Huge chamber of magma (molten rock) beneath the volcano

▶ Pillow lava piles up on the coast of Hawaii, following an eruption of the Kilauea volcano.

MAKE A VOLCANO

You will need:
bicarbonate of soda   a plastic bottle
food colouring   vinegar   sand

Put a tablespoon of bicarbonate of soda in the bottle. Stand it in a tray with a cone of sand around it. Put a few drops of red food colouring in half a cup of vinegar. Pour this into the bottle. In a few moments the volcano should erupt with red, frothy lava.

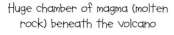

20 **Hot rocks don't always reach the surface.** Huge lumps of rock can rise into the crust and become stuck. These are batholiths. The rock cools slowly and large crystals form. When the crystals cool, they form a rock called granite. In time, the surface of the crust may wear away and the top of the batholith appears above ground.

Boil and bubble

21 **Geysers can be found above old volcanoes.** If volcanoes collapse, the rocks settle above hot rocks in the magma chamber. The gaps between the broken rocks make pipes and chambers. Rain water collects in the chambers, where it heats until it boils. Steam builds up, pushing the water through the pipes and out of an opening called a nozzle. Steam and water shoot up, making a fountain up to 60 metres high.

MAKE A GEYSER

You will need:
bucket   plastic funnel   plastic tubing

Fill a bucket with water. Turn the plastic funnel upside down and sink most of it in the water. Take a piece of plastic tube and put one end under the funnel. Blow down the other end of the tube. A spray of water and air will shoot out of the funnel. Be prepared for a wet face!

22 **In a hot spring, the water bubbles gently to the surface.** As the water is heated in the chamber, it rises up a pipe and into a pool. The pool may be brightly coloured due to tiny plants and animals called algae and bacteria. These live in large numbers in the hot water.

▶ In Iceland, visitors watch the Strokkur geyser erupt.

Clouds of mineral particles forming black smoke

Giant tube worms

Superheated water

Chimney (stack)

▲ The rocky chimneys of a black smoker are built up over time by minerals in the hot water.

24 **Wallowing in a mud pot can make your skin soft.** A mud pot is made when fumes from underground break down rocks into tiny pieces. These mix with water to make mud. Hot gases push through the mud, making it bubble. Some mud pots are cool enough to wallow in.

25 **Steam and smelly fumes can escape from holes in the ground.** These holes are called fumaroles. Since Roman times, people have used the steam from fumaroles for steam baths. The steam may keep joints and lungs healthy.

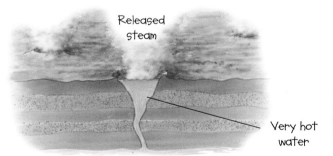

Released steam

Very hot water

▲ Under a fumarole the water gets so hot that it turns to steam, then shoots upwards into the air.

23 **Deep in the ocean are hot springs called black smokers.** They form near rift volcanoes, where magma is close to the ocean floor. Water seeps into cracks in rocks and is heated. The hot water dissolves minerals from the surrounding rock as it travels upwards. The minerals in the water produce dark clouds that look like smoke.

26 **In Iceland, underground steam is used to make lights work.** The steam is sent to power stations and is used to work generators to make electricity. The electricity then flows to homes and powers electrical equipment such as lights, televisions and computers.

Breaking down rocks

27 Ice has the power to break open rocks.
In cold weather, rain water gets into cracks in rocks and freezes. The water expands as it turns to ice. The ice pushes with such power on the rock that it opens up the cracks. Over a long time, a rock can be broken down into thousands of tiny pieces.

▲ Ice has broken through rocks in a creek, forcing the layers apart and breaking off fragments.

28 Living things can break down rocks.
Sometimes a tree seed lands in a crack in a rock. In time, a tree grows and its large roots force open the rock. Tiny living things called lichens dissolve the surface of rocks to reach minerals they need to live. When animals, such as rabbits, make a burrow they may break up some of the rock in the ground.

▼ Tree roots grow in joints in many rocks. As the roots get larger, the rock is forced apart.

29 Warming up and cooling down can break rocks into flakes. When a rock warms up it swells a little. When it cools, the rock shrinks back to its original size. After swelling and shrinking many times, some rocks break up into flakes. Sometimes layers of large flakes form on a rock, making it look like the skin of an onion.

30 Wind can blow a rock to pieces, but it takes a long time. Strong winds hurl dust and sand grains at rock, which slowly break off pieces from the surface, creating strange shapes. It then blows away any tiny loose chips that have formed on the surface of the rock.

▼ Arches National Park in Utah, USA, contains over 2000 natural arches such as this one.

Arch

Region where the glacier forms

Moving ice

◄ On high mountains, glaciers flow downhill until they reach warmer air and start to melt. At the poles, many glaciers flow straight into the sea.

The point where the glacier melts is called the snout

31 Glaciers break up rocks and carry them away. Glaciers are huge pieces of ice that form near mountain tops. They slide slowly down the mountainside. As a glacier moves, some rocks are snapped off and carried along. Others are ground up and carried along as grit and sand.

32 Rocks in rivers and seas are always getting smaller. When water flows over rocks, it gradually wears them down. The water also dissolves minerals from the rock. As well as this, sand and grit in the water slowly grind away the rock surfaces.

I DON'T BELIEVE IT!

In one part of Turkey, people have cut caves in huge cones of rock to make homes.

Settling down

33 Stones of different sizes can combine to make rock. Thousands of years ago, boulders, pebbles and gravel settled on the shores of seas and lakes. Over time, these have become stuck together to make a type of rock called conglomerate. At the foot of cliffs, broken, rocky pieces have collected and joined together to make a rock called breccia.

▲ Pieces of rock can become stuck together by a natural cement to make a lump of larger rock, such as breccia.

▼ These chalk cliffs in Dorset, England have been eroded over time to create sea stacks.

34 Chalk is made from millions of shells and the remains of tiny sea creatures. A drop of sea water contains many microscopic organisms (living things). Some of these have shells. When these organisms die, the shells sink to the seabed and in time form chalk, which builds up to form rocks and cliffs.

35 Limestone is made from seashells. Many kinds of sea animal have a hard shell. When the animal dies, the shell remains on the sea floor. In time, large numbers of shells build up and press together to form limestone. Huge numbers of shells become fossils.

▲ Limestone is usually white, cream, grey or yellow. Caves often form in areas of limestone.

36 If mud is squashed hard enough, it turns to stone. Mud is made from tiny particles of clay and slightly larger particles called silt. When huge layers of mud formed in ancient rivers, lakes and seas, they were squashed by their own weight to make mudstone.

▶ Mudstone has a very smooth surface. It may be grey, black, brown or yellow.

37 Sandstone can be made in the sea or in the desert. When a thick layer of sand builds up, the grains are pressed together and cement forms. This sticks the grains together to make sandstone. Sea sandstone may be yellow with sharp-edged grains. Desert sandstone may be red with round, smooth grains.

◀ Sandstone can form impressive shapes. These pillars in Arches National Park, Utah, USA, are known as the Fins.

I DON'T BELIEVE IT!
Flint is found in chalk and limestone. Thousands of years ago people used flint to make axes, knives and arrow heads.

Uncovering fossils

38 Fossils are formed from animals and plants that were buried. When a plant or animal dies, it is usually eaten by other living things so that nothing remains. If the plant or animal was buried quickly after death, or even buried alive, its body may be preserved.

▼ Prehistoric ocean–dwelling creatures, such as this ichthyosaur, are more likely to leave fossils than those on land.

① The ichthyosaur lives on the ocean floor.

② After death, the ichthyosaur sinks to the seabed. Worms, crabs and other scavengers eat its soft body parts.

③ Sediments cover the hard body parts, such as bones and teeth, which gradually turn into solid rock.

④ Millions of years later the upper rock layers wear away and the fossilized remains are exposed.

39 A fossil is made from minerals. A dead plant or animal can be dissolved by water. An empty space in the shape of the plant or animal is left in the mud and fills with minerals from the surrounding rock.

I DON'T BELIEVE IT!

Some fossils of bacteria are three and a half billion years old.

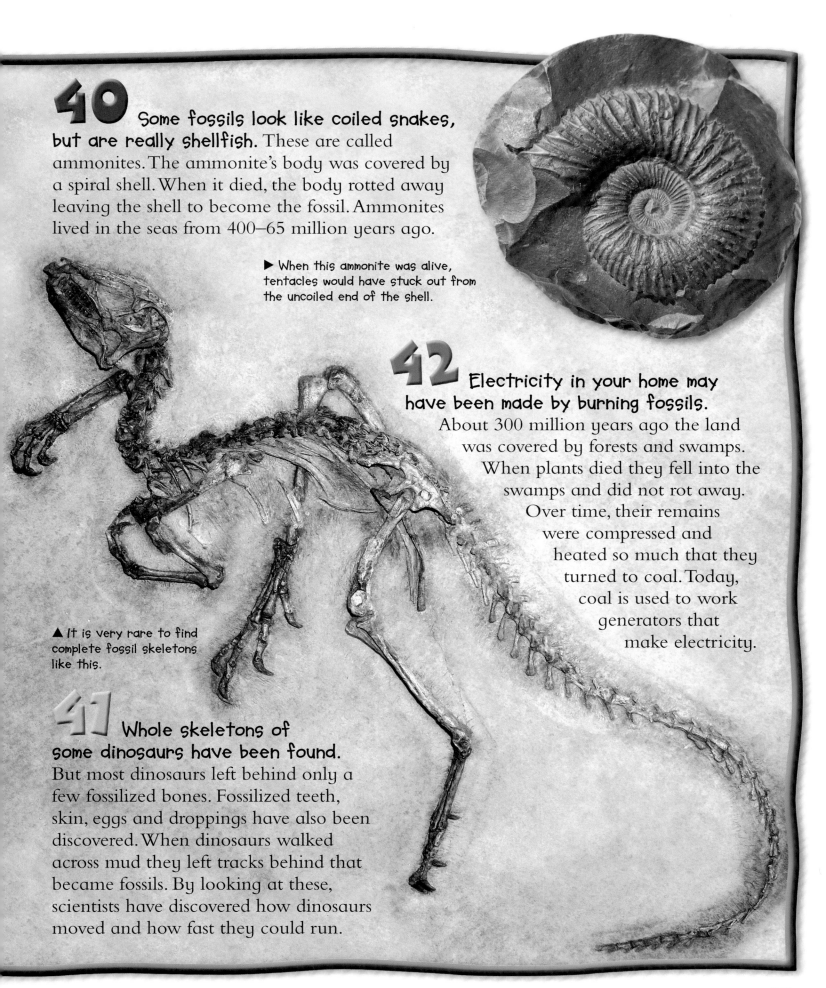

40 **Some fossils look like coiled snakes, but are really shellfish.** These are called ammonites. The ammonite's body was covered by a spiral shell. When it died, the body rotted away leaving the shell to become the fossil. Ammonites lived in the seas from 400–65 million years ago.

▶ When this ammonite was alive, tentacles would have stuck out from the uncoiled end of the shell.

42 **Electricity in your home may have been made by burning fossils.** About 300 million years ago the land was covered by forests and swamps. When plants died they fell into the swamps and did not rot away. Over time, their remains were compressed and heated so much that they turned to coal. Today, coal is used to work generators that make electricity.

▲ It is very rare to find complete fossil skeletons like this.

41 **Whole skeletons of some dinosaurs have been found.** But most dinosaurs left behind only a few fossilized bones. Fossilized teeth, skin, eggs and droppings have also been discovered. When dinosaurs walked across mud they left tracks behind that became fossils. By looking at these, scientists have discovered how dinosaurs moved and how fast they could run.

Rocks that change

43 **When a rock forms in the Earth's crust it may soon be changed again.** There are two main ways this can happen. The rock is heated by hot rocks moving up through the crust, or the crust is squashed and heated as mountains form. Both of these ways make crystals in rock change to form new types of rocks, called metamorphic rock.

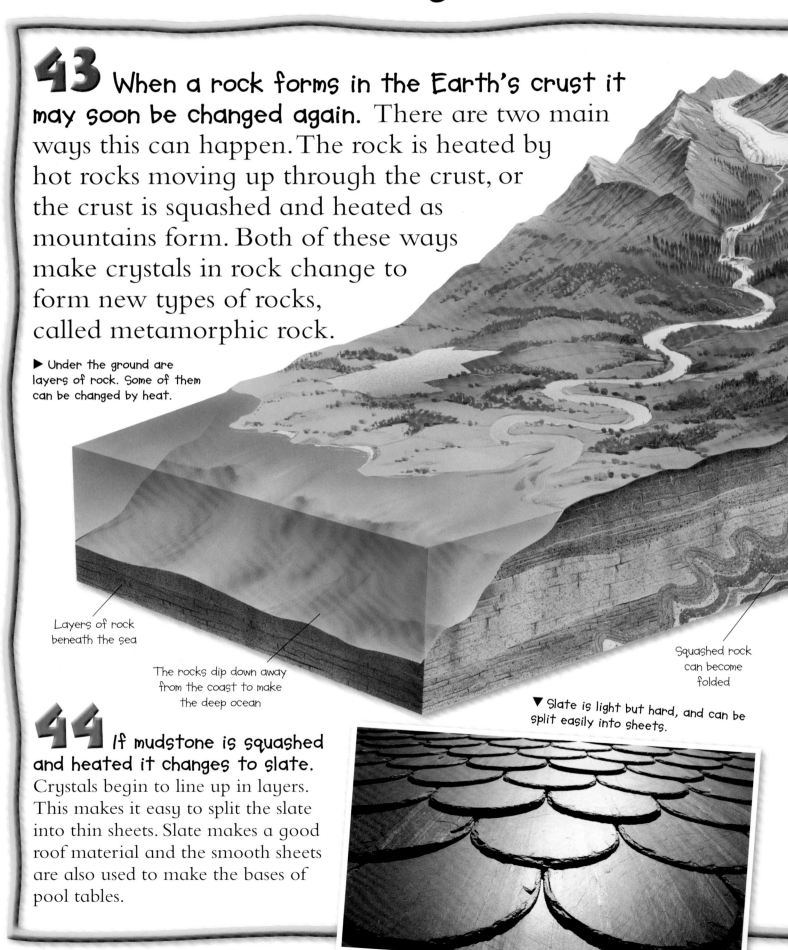

▶ Under the ground are layers of rock. Some of them can be changed by heat.

Layers of rock beneath the sea

The rocks dip down away from the coast to make the deep ocean

Squashed rock can become folded

▼ Slate is light but hard, and can be split easily into sheets.

44 **If mudstone is squashed and heated it changes to slate.** Crystals begin to line up in layers. This makes it easy to split the slate into thin sheets. Slate makes a good roof material and the smooth sheets are also used to make the bases of pool tables.

Some hot rock travels to the surface through the pipe in a volcano

Layers of rock away from the heat remain unchanged

Hot rock trapped in the crust can change the rock around it

46 Rock can become stripy when it is heated and folded. It becomes so hot, it almost melts. Minerals that make up the rock form layers that appear as coloured stripes. These stripes may be wavy, showing the way the rock has been folded. This type of rock is called gneiss (sounds like 'nice'). Gneiss that is billions of years old has been found under volcanoes in Canada.

▼ The stripes in gneiss are formed by layers of different minerals.

▼ Marble is often used to make ornaments like this Egyptian-style cat.

45 If limestone is heated in the Earth's crust it turns to marble. The shells that make up limestone break up when they are heated strongly and form marble, a rock that has a sugary appearance. The surface of marble can be polished to make it look attractive, and it is used to make statues and ornaments.

QUIZ

1. If a sandstone has red, round, smooth grains, where was the sand made?
2. Which rocks are made from seashells and tiny sea creatues?
3. Name six kinds of dinosaur fossil.
4. Which rock changes into slate?

Answers:
1. The desert 2. Limestone and chalk 3. Bones, teeth, skin, eggs, droppings, tracks 4. Mudstone

Massive mountains

47 **The youngest mountains are the highest.** Young mountains have jagged peaks because softer rocks on the top are broken down by weather. The peaks are made from harder rocks that take longer to break down. In time, even these hard rocks are worn away. This makes an older mountain shorter and gives its top a rounded shape.

▶ It takes millions of years for mountains to form, and the process is happening all the time. A group of mountains is called a range. The biggest ranges are the Alps in Europe, the Andes in South America, the Rockies in North America and the highest of all — the Himalayas in Asia.

48 **When plates in the Earth's crust collide, mountains are formed.** When two continental plates push into each other, the crust at the edge of the plates crumples and folds, pushing up mountains ranges. The Himalayan Mountains in Asia formed in this way.

▼ The Himalayan range contains some of the world's highest mountains, including Mount Everest, the highest of all at 8850 metres.

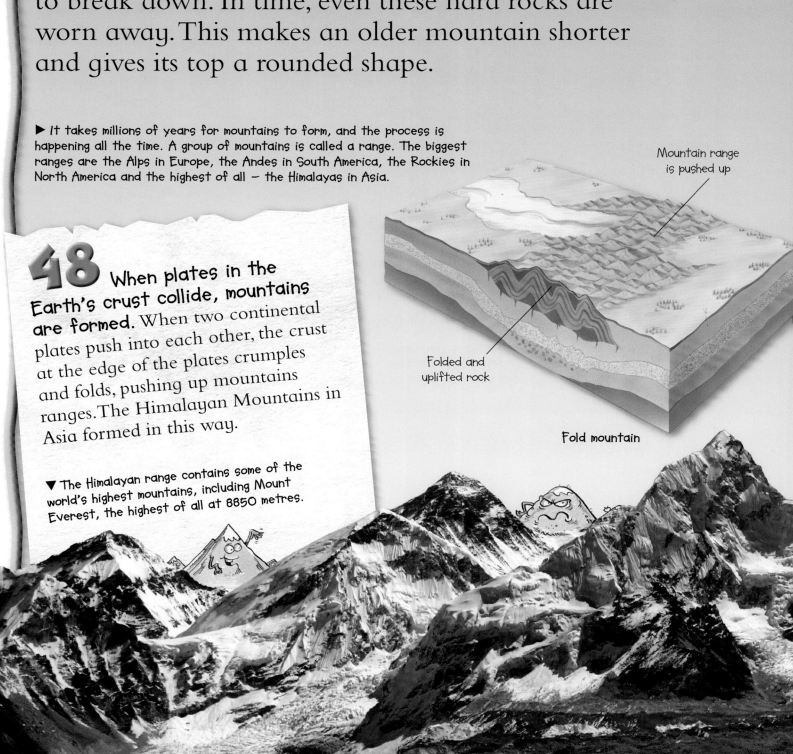

Mountain range is pushed up

Folded and uplifted rock

Fold mountain

49 Some of the Earth's highest mountains are volcanoes. These are formed when molten rock (lava) erupts through the Earth's crust. As the lava cools, it forms a rocky layer. With each new eruption, another layer is added.

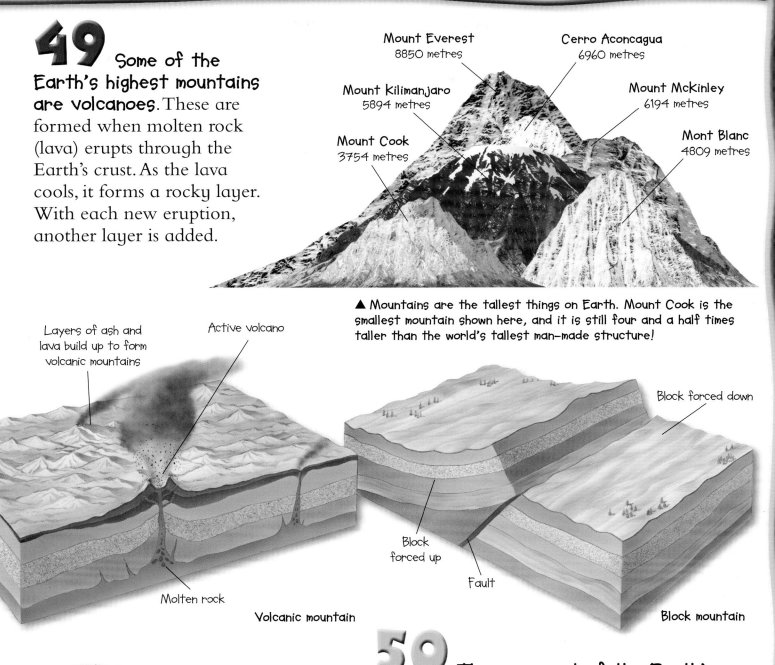

Mount Everest
8850 metres

Cerro Aconcagua
6960 metres

Mount Kilimanjaro
5894 metres

Mount Mckinley
6194 metres

Mount Cook
3754 metres

Mont Blanc
4809 metres

▲ Mountains are the tallest things on Earth. Mount Cook is the smallest mountain shown here, and it is still four and a half times taller than the world's tallest man-made structure!

Layers of ash and lava build up to form volcanic mountains

Active volcano

Molten rock

Volcanic mountain

Block forced down

Block forced up

Fault

Block mountain

MAKE MOUNTAINS

Put a towel on a table top. Place one hand at either end of the towel. Push your hands together slowly and watch miniature fold mountains form.

50 The movement of the Earth's crust can push blocks of rock upwards to make mountains. When the plates in the crust push together, they produce heat which softens the rock, causing it to fold. Farther away from this heat, cooler rock snaps when it is pushed. The snapped rock makes huge cracks called faults in the crust. When a block of rock between faults is pushed by the rest of the crust, it rises to form a block mountain.

Shaking the Earth

51 An earthquake is caused by violent movements in the Earth's crust. Most occur when two plates in the crust move against each other. An earthquake starts deep underground at its 'focus'. Shock waves move out in all directions, shaking the rock. The point where the shock waves reach the surface is called the epicentre. This is where the strongest shaking takes place.

▼ The focus of an earthquake is the point where the plates suddenly move.

Fault line where two plates move against each other

The epicentre is the point on the surface directly above the focus

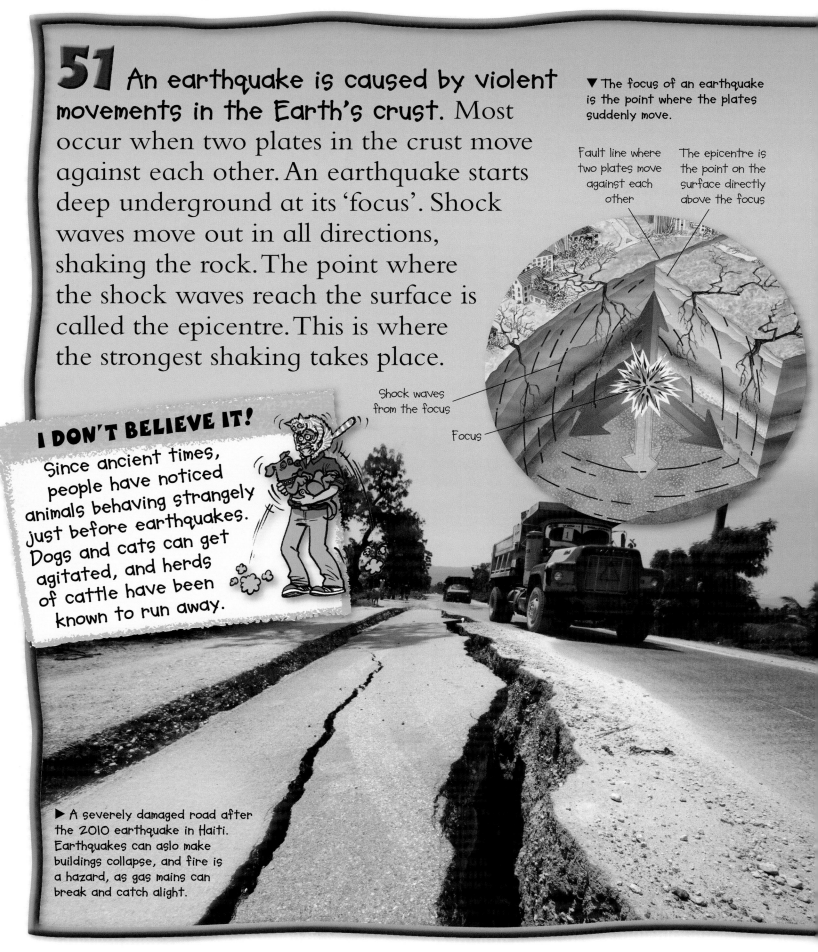

Shock waves from the focus

Focus

I DON'T BELIEVE IT!

Since ancient times, people have noticed animals behaving strangely just before earthquakes. Dogs and cats can get agitated, and herds of cattle have been known to run away.

▶ A severely damaged road after the 2010 earthquake in Haiti. Earthquakes can aslo make buildings collapse, and fire is a hazard, as gas mains can break and catch alight.

52

The power of an earthquake can vary. Half a million earthquakes happen every year but hardly any of these can be felt. About 25 earthquakes each year are powerful enough to cause disasters. Earthquake strength is measured by the Richter Scale. The higher the number on the scale, the more destructive the earthquake.

▼ The Richter Scale measures the strength of the shock waves and energy produced by an earthquake. The shock waves can have little effect, or be strong enough to topple buildings.

Windows break at level 5

Bridges and buildings collapse at level 7

Widespread destruction occurs at level 8

As the tall tsunami reaches shallow water, it surges forwards onto the shore

Decreasing depth slows speed but increases wave height

Upwards wave

An earthquake beneath the sea floor causes a sudden movement of a massive column of water

53

Earthquakes under the sea are called seaquakes. These can cause enormous, devestating waves called tsunamis. As the tsunami rushes across the ocean, it stays quite low. As it reaches the coast, it slows and the water piles up to form a wall. The wave rushes onto the land, destroying everything in its path.

◄ A tsunami can be up to 30 metres high. The weight and power in the wave flattens towns and villages in its path.

Cavernous caves

54 **When rain falls on limestone it becomes a cave-maker.** Rain water can mix with carbon dioxide to form an acid strong enough to attack limestone and make it dissolve. Underground, the action of the rain water makes caves in which streams, waterfalls and lakes can be found.

▼ Rain water flows through the cracks in limestone and makes them wider to eventually form caves. The horizontal caves are called galleries and the vertical caves are called shafts.

Waterfall in a shaft

Gallery

Cave opening

55 **Some caves are made from tubes of lava.** As lava moves down the side of a volcano, its surface cools down quickly. The cold lava becomes solid but below, the lava remains warm and keeps flowing. Under the solid surface a tube may form in which liquid lava flows. When the tube empties, a cave is formed.

► This cave made by lava in Hawaii is so large that people can walk through it without having to bend down.

56 **Dripping water in a limestone cave makes rock spikes.** When water drips from a cave roof it leaves a small amount of limestone behind. A spike of rock begins to form. This rock spike, called a stalactite, grows from the ceiling. Where the drops splash onto the cave floor, tiny pieces of limestone gather. They form a spike which points upwards. This is a stalagmite. Over long periods of time, the two spikes may join together to form a column of rock.

▼ Carlsbad Caverns in New Mexico, USA, are famous for limestone rock formations such as stalactites and stalagmites.

STALACTITES

STALAGMITES

I DON'T BELIEVE IT!

The longest stalactite is 59 metres long. The tallest stalagmite is 32 metres tall.

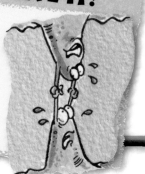

The Earth's treasure

57 Gold can form small grains, large nuggets or veins in rocks. When the rocks wear away, the gold may be found in the sand of river beds. Silver forms branching wires in rock. It does not shine like silver jewellery, but is covered in a black coating called tarnish.

◀ Aluminium must be extracted from its ore — bauxite (shown here) — before it can be used to make all kinds of things, from kitchen foil to aeroplanes.

58 Most metals are found in rocks called ores. An ore is a mixture of different substances, of which metal is one. Each metal has its own ore. For example, aluminium is found in an ore called bauxite. Heat is used to extract metals from their ores. We use metals to make thousands of different things, ranging from watches to jumbo jets.

59 Beautiful crystals can grow in lava bubbles. Lava contains gases which form bubbles. When the lava cools and becomes solid, the bubbles create balloon-shaped spaces in the rock. These are called geodes. Liquids seep into them and form large crystals. The gemstone amethyst forms in this way.

▲ A woman pans for gold in the Mekong River in Southeast Asia.

▲ Inside a geode there is space for crystals to spread out, grow and form perfect shapes.

January
Garnet

February
Amethyst

March
Aquamarine

April
Diamond

May
Emerald

June
Pearl

July
Ruby

August
Peridot

September
Sapphire

October
Opal

November
Topaz

December
Turquoise

60 Gemstones are coloured rocks that cut and polished to make them sparkle. People have used them to make jewellery for thousands of years. Gems such as topaz, emerald and garnet formed in hot rocks that rose to the Earth's crust and cooled. Most are found as small crystals, but a gem called beryl can have a huge crystal – the largest ever found was 18 metres long! Diamond is a gemstone and is the hardest natural substance found on Earth.

▲ There are more than 100 different kinds of gemstone. Some are associated with different months of the year and are known as 'birthstones'. For example, the birthstone for September is sapphire.

MAKE SALT CRYSTALS

You will need:
table salt
magnifying glass
dark-coloured bowl

Dissolve some table salt in some warm water. Pour the salty water into a dark-coloured bowl. Put the bowl in a warm place so the water can evaporate. After a few days, you can look at the crystals with a magnifying glass.

Wild weather

61 **The Earth is wrapped in layers of gases called the atmosphere.** Weather forms in the troposphere, the lowest layer. The layer above is the stratosphere. Planes fly here to avoid bad weather. The mesosphere is the middle layer and above it is the thermosphere. The exosphere reaches to about 960 kilometres above your head, where space begins.

▶ As you travel from Earth's surface into space, you pass through the five layers of the atmosphere.

Orbiting satellite

The auroras

Exosphere
190 to 960 kilometres

Thermosphere
80 to 190 kilometres

Meteors (which burn up in the mesosphere)

Mesosphere
50 to 80 kilometres

Stratosphere
10 to 50 kilometres

Troposphere
0 to 10 kilometres

▼ Water moves continuously between the ocean, air and land in the water cycle.

Water falling as rain

Rain flows into rivers

Water vapour rising from plants

Water vapour rising from the ocean

62 **Clouds are made in the air above the oceans.** When the Sun shines on the water's surface, some evaporates. A gas called water vapour rises into the air. As the vapour cools, it forms clouds which are blown all over the Earth's surface. The clouds cool as they move inland, and produce rain. Rain falls on the land, then flows away in rivers and streams back to the oceans. We call this process the water cycle.

63 A hurricane is a destructive storm which gathers over a warm part of the ocean. Water evaporating from the ocean forms a vast cloud. As cool air rushes in below the cloud, it turns like a huge spinning wheel. The centre of the hurricane (the eye) is completely still. But all around, winds reach speeds of 300 kilometres an hour. If it reaches land the hurricane can blow buildings to pieces.

► A hurricane forms over the surface of a warm ocean, like this one over the Atlantic, but it can move to the coast and onto land.

► A tornado hits the ground in Colorado, USA. The twister hotspot in the American Midwest is known as Tornado Alley.

64 A tornado produces the fastest winds on Earth — it can spin at speeds of up to 480 kilometres an hour. Tornadoes form over ground that has become very warm. Fast-rising air makes a spinning funnel which acts like a high-speed vacuum cleaner. It can devastate buildings and lift up cars, flinging them to the ground.

65 Snowflakes form in the tops of clouds. It is so cold here that water freezes to make ice crystals. As the crystals join together and form larger snowflakes, they fall through the cloud. If the cloud is in warm air, the snowflakes melt and form raindrops. If the cloud is in cold air, the snowflakes reach the ground and begin to settle.

► The ice crystals in a snowflake usually form six arms.

I DON'T BELIEVE IT!
Every day there are 45,000 thunderstorms on Earth. Lightning strikes somewhere in the world about 100 times a second.

Lands of sand and grass

66 The driest places on Earth are deserts. In many deserts there is a short period of rain each year, but some deserts have completely dry weather for many years. The main deserts of the world are shown on the map.

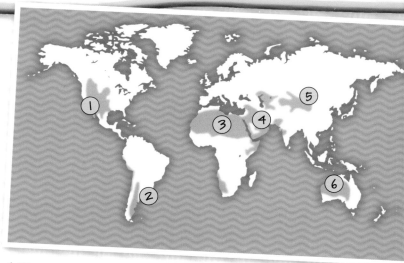

▲ This map shows the major deserts of the world.
① North American deserts – Great Basin and Mojave
② Atacama ③ Sahara ④ Arabian ⑤ Gobi ⑥ Australian deserts – Great Sandy, Gibson, Great Victoria, Simpson

67 Deserts are not always hot. It can be as hot as 50°C in the day but at night the temperature falls as there are less clouds to trap in heat. Deserts near the Equator have hot days all year round but some deserts farther away have very cold winters.

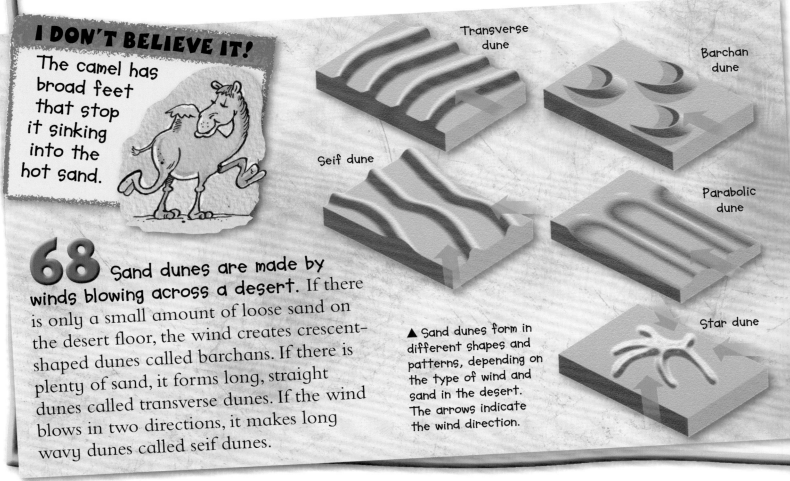

I DON'T BELIEVE IT!
The camel has broad feet that stop it sinking into the hot sand.

Transverse dune

Barchan dune

Seif dune

Parabolic dune

Star dune

▲ Sand dunes form in different shapes and patterns, depending on the type of wind and sand in the desert. The arrows indicate the wind direction.

68 Sand dunes are made by winds blowing across a desert. If there is only a small amount of loose sand on the desert floor, the wind creates crescent-shaped dunes called barchans. If there is plenty of sand, it forms long, straight dunes called transverse dunes. If the wind blows in two directions, it makes long wavy dunes called seif dunes.

71 Grasslands are found in areas where there is more rain than a desert. They are open spaces where trees rarely grow. Tropical grasslands near the Equator are hot all year round. Grasslands farther away have warm summers and cool winters.

72 Large numbers of animals live on grasslands. In Africa, zebras feed on the top of grass stalks, while gnu eat the middle leaves and gazelles feed on the new shoots. This allows all the animals to feed together. Other animals such as lions feed on the plant-eaters.

▲ Plants and animals can thrive at an oasis in the middle of a desert.

69 An oasis is a pool of water in the desert. It forms from rain water that has seeped into the sand and collected in rocks beneath. The water moves through the rock to where the sand is very thin and forms a pool. Trees and plants grow around the pool and animals visit it to drink.

70 A desert cactus stores water in its stem. The grooves on the stem let it swell with water to keep it alive in the dry weather. The spines stop animals biting into the cactus for a drink.

▶ Different animals can live together by eating grass at differing levels. Zebras (1) eat the tall grass. Gnu (2) eat the middle shoots and gazelle (3) graze on the lowest shoots.

Fantastic forests

73 There are three main kinds of forest. They are coniferous, temperate and tropical forests. Each grow in different regions of the world, depending on the climate.

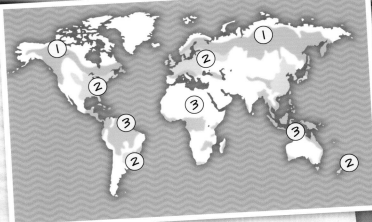

▲ This map shows the major areas of forest in the world:

① Coniferous forest
② Temperate forest
③ Tropical forest

74 Coniferous trees form huge forests around the northern part of the planet. They have long, green, needle-like leaves covered in a waxy coating. These trees stay in leaf throughout the year. In winter, the waxy surface helps snow slide off the leaves so that sunlight can reach them to keep them alive. Coniferous trees produce seeds in cones.

◄ Squirrels can open seed cones from coniferous trees in just a few seconds.

75 Most trees in temperate forests have flat, broad leaves and need large amounts of water to keep them alive. In winter, the trees cannot get enough water from the frozen ground, so they lose their leaves and grow new ones in spring. Deer, rabbits, foxes and mice live on the woodland floor while squirrels, woodpeckers and owls live in the trees.

▲ A jaguar stalks through a dense tropical forest in Belize.

76 Large numbers of trees grow close together in a tropical forest. They have broad, evergreen leaves and branches that almost touch. These form a leafy roof over the forest called a canopy. It rains almost every day in a tropical rainforest. The vegetation is so thick, it can take a raindrop ten minutes to reach the ground. Three-quarters of all known animal and plant species live in rainforests. They include huge spiders, brightly coloured frogs and jungle cats.

▲ The Hoh temperate rainforest in Washington state, USA, is home to elks, bears and cougars.

QUIZ

1. What forms at the top of a cloud?

2. What shape is a barchan sand dune?

3. In which kind of forest would you find brightly coloured frogs?

Answers:
1. Snowflakes 2. Crescent 3. Tropical rainforest

Rivers and lakes

77 **A river can start from a spring.** This is where water flows from the ground. Rain soaks through the ground, and gushes out from the side of a hill. The trickle of water that flows from a spring is called a stream. Many streams join to make a river.

78 **A river changes as it flows to the sea.** Rivers begin in hills and mountains. They are narrow and flow quickly there. When the river flows through flatter land it becomes wider and slow-moving. It makes loops called meanders that may separate and form oxbow lakes. The point where the river meets the sea is the river mouth. This may be a wide channel called an estuary or a group of sandy islands called a delta.

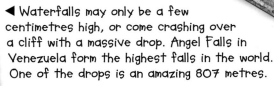

◀ Waterfalls may only be a few centimetres high, or come crashing over a cliff with a massive drop. Angel Falls in Venezuela form the highest falls in the world. One of the drops is an amazing 807 metres.

79 **Water wears rocks down to make a waterfall.** When a river flows from a layer of hard rock onto softer rock, it wears the softer rock down. The rocks and pebbles in the water grind the soft rock away to make a cliff face. At the bottom of the waterfall they make a deep pool called a plunge pool.

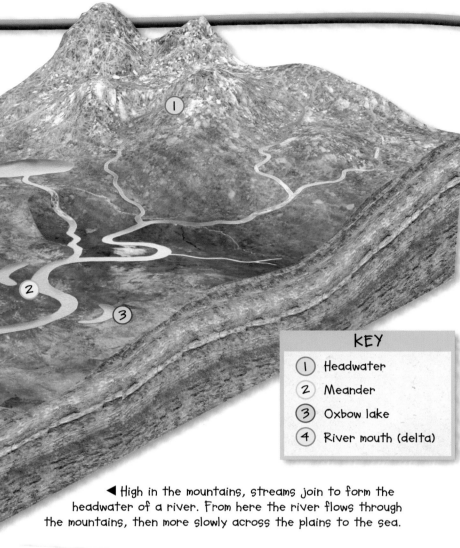

KEY

1. Headwater
2. Meander
3. Oxbow lake
4. River mouth (delta)

◄ High in the mountains, streams join to form the headwater of a river. From here the river flows through the mountains, then more slowly across the plains to the sea.

81 Lakes often form in hollows in the ground. The hollows may be left when glaciers melt or plates in the Earth's crust move apart. Some lakes form when a landslide makes a dam across a river.

▲ A landslide has fallen into the river and blocked the flow of water to make a lake.

82 A lake can form in the crater of a volcano. A few have also formed in craters left by meteorites that hit Earth long ago.

▼ This lake was formed in a volcanic crater.

◄ Most lakes are blue but some are green, pink, red or even white. The Laguna Colorado in Chile is red due to tiny organisms (creatures) that live in the water.

80 Some lake water can be brightly coloured. The colours are made by tiny organisms called algae or by minerals dissolved in the water.

World of water

83 There is so much water on our planet that it could be called 'Ocean' instead of Earth. Only about one-third of the planet is covered by land. The rest is covered by five huge areas of water called oceans. A sea is a smaller area of water within an ocean. For example, the North Sea is part of the Atlantic Ocean and the Malayan Sea is part of the Pacific Ocean.

84 Coasts are always changing. The point where the sea and land meet is called the coast (1). In many places waves crash onto the land and erode it. Caves (2) and arches (3) are punched into cliffs. In time, the arches break and leave columns of rock called sea stacks (4).

◀ The action of the waves gradually erodes the coastline to create different features.

Continental shelf

Continental slope

85 The oceans are so deep that mountains are hidden beneath them. If you paddle by the shore the water is quite shallow, but at its deepest point, the ocean reaches 10,911 metres. The ocean floor is a flat plain with mountain ranges rising across it. These mark where two tectonic plates meet. Nearer the coast are deep trenches where the edges of two plates have moved apart. Extinct volcanoes form mountains called seamounts.

▼ Corals only grow in tropical or sub-tropical waters. They tend to grow in shallow water where there is lots of sunlight.

86 Tiny creatures can make islands in the oceans. Coral is made from the leftover skeletons of sea creatures called polyps. Over millions of years the skeletons build up to form huge coral reefs. Coral also builds up to create islands around extinct volcanoes in the Pacific and Indian Oceans.

87 There are thousands of icebergs floating in the oceans. They are made from glaciers and ice sheets which have formed at the North and South Poles. Only about a tenth of an iceberg can be seen above water. The rest lies below and can damage and sink ships that sail too close.

▶ Under every iceberg is a huge amount of ice, usually much bigger than the area visible from the surface.

| Plain | Oceanic crust | Underwater volcano | Ocean ridge | Deep-sea trench |

▼ Under the oceans are plains and mountains similar to those found on land. There are also long ridges which make new rock on the ocean floor.

The planet of life

88 **There are millions of different kinds of life forms on Earth.** So far, life has not been found anywhere else. Living things survive here because it is warm, there is water and the air contains oxygen. If we discover other planets with these conditions, there may be life on them too.

▼ Despite being the biggest fish in the oceans, the mighty whale shark feeds on tiny shrimp-like creatures.

I DON'T BELIEVE IT!

The star-nosed mole has feelers on the end of its nose. It uses them to find food.

▼ This caterpillar eats as much plant life as possible before beginning its change to a butterfly.

89 **Many living things on the Earth are tiny.** They are so small that we cannot see them. A whale shark is the largest fish on the planet, yet it feeds on tiny shrimp-like creatures. These in turn feed on even smaller plant-like organisms called plankton, which make food from sunlight and sea water. Microscopic bacteria are found in the soil and even on your skin.

90 **Animals cannot live without plants.** A plant makes food from sunlight, water, air and minerals in the soil. Animals cannot make their own food so many of them eat plants. Others survive by eating the plant-eaters. If plants died out, all the animals would die too.

91 **The air can be full of animals.** On a warm day, clouds of midges and gnats form close to the ground. In spring and autumn, flocks of birds fly to different parts of the world to nest. On summer evenings bats hunt for midges flying in the air.

92 **The surface of the ground is home to many small animals.** Mice scurry through the grass. Larger animals such as deer hide in bushes. The elephant is the largest land animal. It does not need to hide because few animals would attack it.

93 **If you dig into the ground you can find animals living there.** The earthworm is a common creature found in the soil. It feeds on rotting plants that it pulls into the soil. Earthworms are eaten by moles that dig their way underground.

▲ Animals thrive in many different kinds of habitats on Earth. The skies, the ground and even underground are home to countless forms of life.

Caring for the planet

94 **Many useful materials come from the Earth.** These make clothes, buildings, furniture and containers such as cans. Some materials, like those used to make buildings, last a long time. Others, such as those used to make cans, may be used up on the day they are bought.

Factories pump out chemicals that can cause acid rain. They also dump polluted water in rivers amd seas.

95 **We may run out of some materials in the future.** Metals are found in rocks called ores. When all the ore has been used up we will not be able to make new metal. We must be careful not to use too much wood, as although new trees are always being planted, they may not grow fast enough for our needs, and we could run out.

96 **We can make materials last longer by recycling them.** Metal, glass and plastic are often thrown away and buried in a tip after they have been used. Today more people recycle materials. This means sending them back to factories to be used again.

◀ Sorting waste into different materials before it is collected makes recycling more efficient.

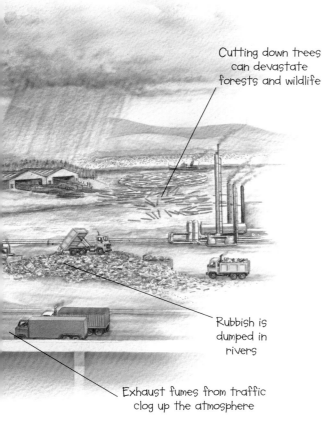

▼ Here are some of the ways in which we are harming our planet today. We must think of better ways to treat the Earth in the future.

Cutting down trees can devastate forests and wildlife

Rubbish is dumped in rivers

Exhaust fumes from traffic clog up the atmosphere

97 Air and water can be polluted by our activities.
Burning coal and oil for electricity makes fumes which can make rain water acidic. This can kill trees and damage soil. Chemicals from factories are sometimes released into rivers and seas, endangering wildlife.

98 Living things can be protected.
Large areas of land have been made into national parks where wildlife is protected. People can come to study, observe and enjoy plants and animals.

99 We use huge amounts of fuel.
The main fuels are coal and oil, which are used to make electricity. Oil is also used in petrol for cars. In time, these fuels will run out. Scientists are developing ways of using other energy sources such as wind power. Huge wind turbines are already used to make electricity.

100 The Earth is nearly five billion years old.
From a ball of molten rock it has grown into a living, breathing planet. We must try to keep it that way. Switching off lights to save energy and picking up litter are things we can all do to protect our planet.

▶ In a wind turbine, the spinning movement is changed into electrical energy.

I DON'T BELIEVE IT!
By the middle of the 21st century 30 to 50 percent of all living species may be extinct.

Index

Entries in **bold** refer to main subject entries. Entries in *italics* refer to illustrations.